Nations at Rage!

Abraham 'Wole Haastrup

Nations at Rage!

Abraham 'Wole Haastrup

Published in Australia by
Sunrise Foundation International (SFI).

Nations at Rage!
Copyright @ 2016

Abraham 'Wole Haastrup

ISBN 978–0–992-3823-4-6

All rights reserved. No part of this book may be produced, stored in a retrieval system, or transmitted in any form or by any means – electronic, mechanical, photocopy, recording, scanning, or any other – except for brief quotations in printed reviews, without the permission of the Publisher.

Unless otherwise indicated, Scripture quotations are from The New King James Version of the Holy Bible, copyright 1982 – Thomas Nelson, Inc. used by permission.

Published in Melbourne, Australia
by Sunrise Foundation International (SFI).

Printed in Australia

Other Books by the same author:

- God Still Speaks Today

- High Praise

- Obedience- The Secret of Miracles

- In Remembrance of Me

- Your Last Hope

- The Secret of Divine Favour

- The Christian Worker

- Ebenezer (God Can Do It Again)

- The Almighty Formulae

TABLE OF CONTENTS

Introduction

Part I : God's Redemptive Purpose and Plan

1. Redemptive Gifts and Wealth of Nations
2. International Conspiracy
3. Identity Crises
4. Abuse - The Danger of Distorted Identity

Part II: A Reprobate Generation

5. Homosexuality – The core issues
6. Homosexuality - The Responses of The Church
7. Homosexuality - the Doom of Nations
8. The Light Shines in Darkness

Part III: Peace In A Convulsing World

9. Inter-Faith Dialogue and World Peace
10. A Convulsing World
11. In a Time Like this

    Acknowledgements

(Psalm 2:1-5)

1 "Why do the heathen rage, and the people imagine a vain thing? 2 The kings of the earth set themselves, and the rulers take counsel together, against the LORD, and against his anointed, saying, 3 Let us break their bands asunder, and cast away their cords from us. 4 HE that sitteth in the heavens shall laugh: the Lord shall have them in derision. 5 Then shall he speak unto them in his wrath, and vex them in his sore displeasure."

INTRODUCTION

We are in perilous times. It is a season in which Nations are at rage! Nations, their leaders, their systems, and their creativities are all at rage. They are at rage against the Living God. Nations are at rage against God's righteous laws, His orders, and His institutions, especially the family and the Church. Nations are at rage - ascribing to and claiming that man himself is the 'primary cause' of existence rather than a 'secondary cause'. Man now thinks that he - an ordinary dust of the earth and a mere vapor (- which is there in the morning but gone in the wake of the sun), is accountable to no higher One but himself!

Nations are also at rage against God's Son, JESUS CHRIST OF NAZARETH - the Saviour and Hope of the World. Nations are at rage against His Name, His Kingdom agenda, against His atoning sacrifice on the Cross, and His Redemptive purpose and plan.

It is interesting that Nations are also at rage against themselves - warring and terrorizing each other through political, socio-economic, religious and technological wars. The times we are in have been accurately foretold & described in the Bible by our Lord Jesus. Apostle Paul also alerted men a long time ago about what we are seeing today (see Matthew 24:1-end, I Tim 4:1-3; II Tim 3:1-7;Rom 1: 28-32).

The word "rage" has been defined in various ways. It is said to be 'a strong feeling of anger that is difficult to control'; or 'a sudden expression of violent anger'. It is also described as: 'to talk in an extremely angry way - to shout loudly and angrily'.

Finally, rage is an action or reaction that 'happens or continues in a destructive, violent, or an intense way'.

In short, the word 'rage' can be summarized as 'an outpouring of pent-up anger through words and actions'. Often, violence accompanies it.

The raging of Nations is multi-dimensional: it covers National and International actions, as well as rebellious policies and operations of leaders and intelligential against the God of Heaven and Earth. However, God - the Maker, Creator an Sustainer of all, can no longer fold His hands or tolerate man's arrogance, flagrant, wanton disregard of His person and laws. He must act and react from His Throne in Heaven! The aftermath of God's action and reaction from Heaven, against all unrighteousness of men have been in the form of natural calamities and misfortunes which befall Nations - their lands, their people, their leaders, and their future. The sufferings, confusions and troubles that men will begin (or have begun) to experience as a result of the evil they have sown by denying God (- His existence, ownership and Lordship of the whole universe) - over the years, all abound around us.

On the pages of this Book, you will be informed, provoked, and challenged. Please don't let it end there. Let what you discover propel you to concrete and urgent action that will result in saving yourself, your loved ones, and as many as possible of this generation that seems so desperate to waste itself!

PART 1:

GOD'S REDEMPTIVE PURPOSE AND PLAN

CHAPTER 1

REDEMPTIVE GIFTS AND WEALTH OF NATIONS

As God has purposes and plans for individuals, and He has duly endowed us with gifts to fulfill such purposes & plans, so it is with Nations. For every Nation on earth, God has a redemptive purpose. He also has a grand plan. To assist in fulfilling their purposes, God has endowed Nations with vast resources - natural, physical, human, even spiritual & cultural (Deut 32:7-8; Acts 17:28-31). To some, God gave strategic geographical locations. To others, God gave special mineral deposits. To some yet others, God gave a huge land mass with high population. In some lands, God allowed a good number of special talents and creative abilities. Of course, to some Nations also, God gave technological breakthroughs. To some Nations, God even gave rich and fruitful soil where virtually anything could grow and thrive. Unfortunately, due to sin, human selfishness, exploitation and in some cases gross ignorance, some Nations abused, wasted and destroyed their own God-given resources. Equally, as the devil is renown and out in his three-fold assignment to steal, kill and destroy individuals (- so as to pervert their destinies), so he does to Nations. He corrupts, disrupts and destroys the good things God has endowed Nations with.

The effect of all these is that many a Nation are in serious and abject poverty, and want. A greater percentage of the population of some countries are virtually begging to live. On the other hand, even the so-called Rich and advanced Nations have become morally decadent, and are stinking to the heavens! The good news however, is that in the ultimate, whether men like it or not, God's perfect will must come to pass (Psalm 33:8-12).

CHAPTER 2

INTERNATIONAL CONSPIRACY

For several decades now, a subtle international conspiracy had been on. It has affected the whole world and our atmosphere - both physically and spiritually. The so called 'world powers' had been on conquests, and in alliance they have formed 'Blocs' and 'Cartels' against the 'weak nations'. The goal of the 'strong' had been to exploit and super-impose themselves on virtually all facets of human existence in the 'weak' nations - their economy, education, social, military, industries, exploration and exploitation of mineral and natural resources, as well as price determination, etc.

Without any doubt, and probably unknown to the 'exploiter' and the 'exploited', there are spiritual dimensions and undertone to the whole matter. For example, I was made to understand that some viruses were created in laboratories of the western Nations and sent to the atmospheres of the developing world so as to engineer crises for the poor Nations, and then create markets for the super-powers. Not only this, it has been made clear that many wars - whether political, tribal, or even religious - are remotely engineered by the super powers to destabilize governments of the LDCs and create markets for arms and ammunitions made in the Advanced Nations! Often, much of the purported aids and help to these nations have been with strings which in many cases licensed the super powers to dictate terms of trade and acquisition of patent rights over mining, refining and pricing of resources that originate in the developing nations. Some nations, it is understood, have had their mineral reserves sold to and paid for by the developed nations at so ridiculous prices to the extent that for the next 100 YEARS, such resources must be mined and carted away to foreign lands!

While one may not lay all the blame at the door steps of these developed nations, the selfishness of political class, intellectual, and business leaders of these less developed nations who sell their birthright as well as the destiny of many unborn generations had helped to further complicate the matter.

At the dawn of the decade 1990-1999, the world was divided into two: Debtor versus Creditor Nations. During that period, a particular highly populated and oil-rich African Country south of the Sahara was asked by the IMF to stop measuring its wealth in terms of *per capital Income* (PCI), but in terms of debt per capital (DPC). This was because the IMF had projected that every child that came into the world in that African Nation between 1990 and1999 was already owing $US1,500.00 at birth! Today, almost twenty-five years after, that Nation and many others in Africa are yet to be debt-free in the real sense of it.

CHAPTER 3

IDENTITY CRISES

'Then the word of the LORD came to me, saying: "Before I formed you in the womb I knew you; Before you were born, I sanctified you; I ordained you a prophet to the Nations'" (Jer 1:4-5)

One of the things the devil is very good at is deception. He manifests this evil character through the art of impersonation. Satan is also a strong manipulator. Often, he succeeds in discrediting and devaluing man. Many a people especially the Youths are victims of this vital tool of Satan. The Devil, using technology, some sections of the media, as well as the entertainment, music and sports industries, had succeeded in telling our young ones that they are a 'dot' - a meaningless, loveless and unwanted nonentity who is just roaming in a versed world. He told them also that they are of no consequence, and had no meaning or purpose whatsoever for living. Unfortunately many Youths are living to fulfill that mould. There is no lie that can ever be greater that this.

Are you a Youth? Have you been under such deception? Have you been fed-up with living, and even contemplated terminating your God-given life? PLEASE DON'T! Hear and listen: YOU ARE NOT 'DOT'! You are a special creature of God. God loves you. God made you in His image and likeness. God has a very great purpose and plan for your existence. Not only these, God has endowed you with vast resources that are waiting discovery and release! All these are clearly stated in God's WORD - the Bible. Perhaps the greatest disservice the Devil and his agents have done to you is to make you to hate the God of the Bible as well as His word. These satanic agents know quiet well that in the Bible you will discover the truth about God and about your real self!

There was a young folk like you who once lived. He too initially thought life was without meaning and purpose. Then one day he had an encounter that straightened him up. Hear him:

> *"Then the word of the LORD came unto me, saying, Before I formed thee in the belly I knew thee; and before thou camest forth out of the womb I sanctified thee, and I ordained thee a prophet unto the nations."*

It was a life-changing experience and he was never the same again. By your reading this book, may you encounter your Maker, and may your life receive a fresh light and meaning in Jesus Name. This will happen if and when you invite Jesus into your heart or you give your life to Him. The moment you do so, the light of God will flood your soul. Thereafter, your life will begin to have a true meaning, and take shape. Ephesians 2:8-10 (NLT), reads:

> *"God saved you by his grace when you believed. And you can't take credit for this; it is a gift from God. Salvation is not a reward for the good things we have done, so none of us can boast about it. For we are God's masterpiece. He has created us anew in Christ Jesus, so we can do the good things he planned for us long ago."*

This statement is also very true of you. You are a masterpiece! God took time to fabricate you. His plan is to make a STAR out of you. He wants to showcase you to your generation. By His grace, I am now an adult. I make bold to say that three-quarters of what I now know about myself, and my future, had been discovered through reading and studying God's Word - the Holy Bible. In it, I came to know God - His personality, His love, mercy, and trustworthiness. I also came to know God's redemptive purpose for my life, and how great a plan He has for me. I am still discovering more and more about Him and about myself. You too can!

Hear me once again: YOU ARE NOT AN ACCIDENT OF NATURE. YOU DO NOT JUST OCCUR. GOD INTENTIONALLY AND SPECIALLY FASHIONED YOU! (IPeter 2:9-10).

YOU NEED TO DISCOVER YOUR TRUE AND GREAT IDENTITY! Until you do, you will continue to be a shadow of your real self, and waste a great destiny that God has in mind for you. Never in such a state will you ever be fulfilled or be happy.

> *"And ye shall know the truth, and the truth shall make you free. If the Son therefore shall make you free, ye shall be free indeed."*

Chapter 4

Abuse - The Danger of Distorted Identity

It has often been said that ignorance leads to abuse. One of the dangers of a distorted identity is abuse! Many a man, woman, boy, girl, a husband, wife or even a parent are abusing themselves through wrong and unhealthy ways of living - all because they have no true knowledge of who God made them to be.

The story is told in Max Lucado's book "You Are Special", of a young boy Punchinello - a wooden person in a village of wooden people. The villagers had a practice of sticking stars on achievers & dots on strugglers. Punchinello had so many dots that the people gave him dots for no reason at all. But when he (Punchinello) met Eli, his Maker, Eli affirmed him, telling him to disregard the opinion of others. "I made you" he explained, "and I don't make mistakes". Punchinello had never heard such words. When he did, his dots began to drop off!

Today, open the Bible and get God's opinion of you, and begin to build your life on it. It is the only opinion that counts** Isa 54:10 says:

> "For the mountains shall depart, and the hills be removed; but my kindness shall not depart from thee, neither shall the covenant of my peace be removed, saith the LORD that hath mercy on thee."

What are we trying to say here? The secret behind all and every form of abuse - from substance and drug abuse, to prostitution, child trafficking, sexual perversions (homosexuality, lesbianism, gay, bestiality, trans-gender, tattooing, etc), including suicide bombing and terrorism, is ignorance. This ignorance is fueled by Satan's destructive manipulations (John 10:10).

In the next four chapters, we will focus on one of the greatest manifestations of abuse that arose out of a distorted identity.

PART II:

A REPROBATE GENERATION

CHAPTER 5

HOMOSEXUALITY – THE CORE ISSUES

In II Timothy 2:16-19, 25-26, the Bible says:

> *"But shun profane and idle babbling, for they will increase unto more ungodliness. And their message will spread like cancer. Hymenaeus and Philetus are of this sort, who have strayed concerning the truth, saying the resurrection is already past; and they overthrow the faith of some. Nevertheless the solid foundation of God stands, having this seal: "The Lord knows those who are His", and "Let everyone who names the name of Christ depart from iniquity"… In humility correcting those who are in opposition, if God perhaps will grant them repentance, so that they may know the truth, and that they may come to their senses and escape the snare of the devil, having being taken captive by him to do his will".*

In our end-time generation, words like 'prostitution', 'homosexuality', 'lesbianism', 'bestiality', etc. have gradually entered our vocabulary. Modernism, Liberalists agenda, and sin in general, have opened men and women to all forms of abnormal sexual relationships - between same sexes - men with men, women with women; and between man or woman and animals!

Today, especially in the Western world, homosexuals, lesbians, and gay marriage in particular, have gained momentum. These people have 'come out'. They are no more in the closets. Through TV, Radio, Newspapers, Magazines, Internet, etc., they are preaching their doctrine of human right, tolerance, equality, justice and love. They do not want to be perceived as abnormal, insane or dangerous. They want to be recognized and accepted socially, politically, and even spiritually. It is another element of rage! The key issue behind this evil manifestation of rage is 'Reprobacy'. In Romans 1:18-32, the Bible says:

> *"For the wrath of God is revealed from heaven against all ungodliness and unrighteousness of men, who suppress the truth in unrighteousness, [19] because what may be known of God is manifest in them, for God has shown it to them. [20] For since the creation of the world His invisible attributes are clearly seen, being understood by the things that are made, even His eternal power and Godhead, so that they are without excuse, [21]*

because, although they knew God, they did not glorify Him as God, nor were thankful, but became futile in their thoughts, and their foolish hearts were darkened. [22] Professing to be wise, they became fools, [23] and changed the glory of the incorruptible God into an image made like corruptible man—and birds and four-footed animals and creeping things. [24] Therefore God also gave them up to uncleanness, in the lusts of their hearts, to dishonor their bodies among themselves, [25] who exchanged the truth of God for the lie, and worshiped and served the creature rather than the Creator, who is blessed forever. Amen. [26] For this reason God gave them up to vile passions. For even their women exchanged the natural use for what is against nature. [27] Likewise also the men, leaving the natural use of the woman, burned in their lust for one another, men with men committing what is shameful, and receiving in themselves the penalty of their error which was due. [28] And even as they did not like to retain God in their knowledge, God gave them over to a debased mind, to do those things which are not fitting; [29] being filled with all unrighteousness, sexual immorality, wickedness, covetousness, maliciousness; full of envy, murder, strife, deceit, evil-mindedness; they are

> *whisperers, [30] backbiters, haters of God, violent, proud, boasters, inventors of evil things, disobedient to parents, [31] undiscerning, untrustworthy, unloving, unforgiving, unmerciful; [32] who, knowing the righteous judgment of God, that those who practice such things are deserving of death, not only do the same but also approve of those who practice them."*

The foregoing text speaks volume - both to sex perverters and their promoters, as well as to the Church. Reprobacy is a very dangerous thing. A reprobate mind is a debased, depraved, and demoralized. It is also a mind that has been perverted and turned backwards and/or upside down. It is a mind whose eyes of understanding have been closed and whose sensitivity to both spiritual, mental, emotional and moral issues have become zero. The conscience of such a man or woman has become dead. In effect, he or she can hardly know right from left. He or she is a walking corpse, so to say!

The Triplet-evil of our time

When an individual, a family or nation forsakes God, evil will overtake them. There had been many evils in our generation, but perhaps the greatest so far are abortion, homosexuality (and its attendant Gay marriage), and very lately, religious fundamentalism and terrorism. Since, our pre-occupation in this Section of this book is homosexuality, we will not go into discussing the issue of abortion. Suffice it to say here that the God of the Bible is the giver and source of life, and He frowns at destruction of innocent lives, no matter the circumstances of the conception of that new life.

In our age or season, we have several indicators of reprobate minds – all working through reprobate organizations, government apparatus, as well as political and academic leaders. Among other things, Abortion, Homosexuality, Lesbianism, Bestiality, Gay marriage, Nudity, Religious fanaticism, ritual and suicide killings, and of course Terrorism, and such likes, are manifestations of reprobacy.

It can be disheartening to know how pervading these evils have been in our generation. More disheartening is realizing how much of this evil has crept into the Church. Satan - the arch enemy of the Church and the Cross of Christ is behind it all. A deep search of the Scriptures reveal that the UNCHANGING God has already said a lot in His Word, the Holy Bible on the subject of sexual perversion.

The attitude or stand of various segments of the Church, as well as the danger of the Church being silent at this greatest evil of our generation, are part of what we are considering in this Section. Of course, the crucial need for the Church to take a righteous stand and response is also discussed.

"Homosexuality" has been defined as an "erotic activity with another of same sex. It is also to refer to sexual relationship or intercourse between persons of the same sex – man with man. When the relationship is between a woman and another woman, it is called lesbianism. Both homosexuality and lesbianism are perversions of God's original plan and arrangement. God frowned, and still frowns at it, and has pronounced some curses not only on those who do them but also on all who promote them ?2. For example, Rom 1:32; I Cor 6:9-10 declare:

> *"^{32} Who knowing the judgment of God, that they which commit such things are worthy of death, not only do the same, but have pleasure in them that do them....^{9} Know ye not that the unrighteous shall not inherit the kingdom of God? Be not deceived: neither fornicators, nor idolaters, nor adulterers, nor effeminate, nor abusers of themselves with mankind, ^{10} Nor thieves, nor covetous, nor drunkards, nor revilers, nor extortioners, shall inherit the kingdom of God."*

Understanding Homosexuality (behavior and practice)

The bastardly act of Homosexuality can be said to be one of those long term effects of the Fall of man in the Garden of Eden. Man rejected God and refused to accept and follow the truth. Claiming to be wise, man became distorted in his mind, vain in his imagination, lustful in his heart, and inordinate in his affections.3 The Bible described the mind that yields to sexual perversion as 'reprobate'. In addition to what we said earlier in this chapter, a reprobate mind is a distorted mind. It is a mind that breaks laws - both natural and spiritual! It cannot recognize evil or refrain from it. Worse still, when such a mind is involved in acts injurious to himself or herself, it cannot refrain from it.

Promotion of Homosexuality (The power of money & politics)

In today's world, there is virtually nothing left that has not been done by supporters and promoters of homosexuality. They seek legal protection for their trade. They want their views taught in schools, they present their ungodly acts in literatures and electronic media, they use advocacy groups to lobby parliaments. They hide under and use NGOs, financial aids in LDCs, and even church leaders to promote their evil intentions. Of course, in their evil bid they have gone to the ridiculous extent of placating and blackmailing true and righteous church leaders who stand firm upon God's Word, the Holy Bible and it's declarations against the subject and acts of homosexuality. In short, they try to use the power of money, intellect, and politics to fight God's written Word, the Holy Bible, and in effect fight GOD Himself. But it is an exercise in futility! (See Lam 3:37).

The Humanistic & Liberalist Agenda

Humanism is an ethical philosophy that prioritizes universal human qualities and intellect. It is empowered by rationalism. Humanism rejects the validity of transcendental justifications such as dependence on faith, the supernatural or divinely revealed truths.

Greek philosophy and philosophers were the intellectual source of this way of thinking, but it came to dominate the Western societies in the Enlightenment of the 18th Century which emphasized human reason as the only source of knowledge. Demonic principalities and powers referred to in the Bible as "the spiritual wickedness in high places" are of course, behind these 'isms':

> *"[10] Finally, my brethren, be strong in the Lord, and in the power of his might. [11] Put on the whole armour of God, that ye may be able to stand against the wiles of the devil. [12] For we wrestle not against flesh and blood, but against principalities, against powers, against the rulers of the darkness*

of this world, against spiritual wickedness in high places. ¹³ Wherefore take unto you the whole armour of God, that ye may be able to withstand in the evil day, and having done all, to stand...³ For though we walk in the flesh, we do not war after the flesh: ⁴ (For the weapons of our warfare are not carnal, but mighty through God to the pulling down of strong holds;) ⁵ Casting down imaginations, and every high thing that exalteth itself against the knowledge of God, and bringing into captivity every thought to the obedience of Christ;" (Ephes 6:10-13; II Cor 10:3-5).

Mainstream liberalism is the political cover for both humanism and atheism. Radical (as against conservative liberalism) allows you to theoretically believe in God without having to accept any of His standards (e.g., sanctity of life, sex only within heterosexual marriage - as against homosexual, etc.). Liberalism keeps introducing new and improved versions of a 'God' whose moral standards seem to fit the preferences of liberal society.

The problem with humanism and liberalism is that they engender much philosophical hypocrisy. The same people who espouse total sexual freedom in the choice of partners and genders are also the most vocal voices of shock and outrage at the number of child sex slaves (pedophiles), and HIV/AIDS orphans in the world. They are living in denial of the fact that the so-called freedoms they espouse are a primary cause of the very things they outrage about. <u>In humanism, God is meant to orbit around man – if He exists at all</u> [4.] The truth however is, once the creature ceases to orbit around his/her Creator, he or she is lost!

Where do all these fit into our discussion on Homosexuality? As part of its grand design or plan, Satan and his agents had penetrated, polluted, distorted, & divided the leadership of the two most populous Christian organizations globally – the Catholic Church and the Anglican Church. He, Satan had pressured them into succumbing to the evil agenda called humanism. Through it, satan aims at destroying the very foundation of society – Godly and Biblical marriages - i.e., marriage between a man and woman (Gen 2:18-24; Matt 19:3-10).

Over time, natural and normal children will rarely be produced, and the earth will be populated by Clones – faithless, conscienceless, artificial men and women who they can robotically control and make to do whatever their grand master, Satan inspires them to do. Whether the devil likes it or not, the truth however remains: There is God. He is active in the affairs of men (Dan 4:1-3, 34-37). This God has definite standards of moral conduct. Everyman must choose to embrace Him, or he/she will face His wrath![5]

The grand agenda of liberalism is therefore to contest

God's ownership of man, and to root out from man's heart, the fear of God, thereby making man faithless, driven by lusts of the flesh and pride of life, and a - ready tool in Satan's hands!

The Bible and Homosexuality

Concerning our subject matter, one could ask many questions. For example, "Where and when did the now-pervasive evil called homosexuality start"? "Had the Bible ever said anything about it"? And, if it had, "what has it said"? "Are people aware of what the Bible says"? Finally, "are those who know what the Bible said about all forms of sexual perversions taking it serious"?

The whole of Chapter 18 of the Book of Leviticus is centered on God's laws vis-a-vis sexual morality. In particular, Vs 22 says:

> *"You shall NOT lie with a man as with a woman. It is an abomination"!*

Also, I Cor 6: 9-10, declares:

> *"⁹ Know ye not that the unrighteous shall not inherit the kingdom of God? Be not deceived: neither fornicators, nor idolaters, nor adulterers, nor effeminate, nor abusers of themselves with mankind, 10 Nor thieves, nor covetous, nor*

drunkards, nor revilers, nor extortioners, shall inherit the kingdom of God." (See Luke 16:15)

That a large section of the mainstream and orthodox Church is wasting its precious time & resources trying to pamper, condone or tolerate this great evil which the Devil has been promoting to destroy humanity, and the sanctity of the Church (the body of Christ), is still a mystery! Our Lord Jesus Himself (in Matt 16:6-12), and Apostle Paul also (in I Cor 5:6), warned that:

"A little leaven leaveneth the loaf"!

Post-Christian Society

By Post – Christian Society, we refer to the Western world. In terms of true and Biblical Christianity, it can be said that this is a backslidden world. Though materially wealthy, and technologically advanced, the Western world has had its values inverted. Unlike the men of Jericho in II Kings 2:19-21 (who, realizing that things were not what they should be, and being unable to pin-point the basic causes of the problem, ran to Elisha the man of God), leaders in the West, both political and religious, appear blinded to the decadence and spiritual barrenness in their lands. Another important characteristic of this 'new world' is their trying to remove the idea of God out of the minds of their citizenry? Governments' economic, political, educational, social and even work-related policies are anti-Bible or anti-Christian. In the last 20-25 years, these Nations have taken God (and His life-shaping Word - the Holy Bible), prayers, as well as moral instructions out of their school curricular, and also, out of their national constitutions!

CHAPTER 6

HOMOSEXUALITY:
(THE RESPONSES OF THE CHURCH)

The mere mention of the word "Church" brings several images to many minds. Some think of buildings with artistically painted windows, pews on the inside, and the cemetery located a little off its courtyards. Some reminisce memories of when Mom and Dad took them as young children to Sunday School classes. The Church is far beyond buildings or even the congregations inside them.

The Church is a Biblical institution with Christ as the Head. She was birthed at Pentecost, and given to the world to showcase the reality of the Person, Ministry and Power in the Name of Jesus Christ. It is made up of 'the called-out' individuals. In Matt 16:18-19, Our Lord Jesus said:

> *"[18] And I say also unto thee, That thou art Peter, and upon this rock I will build my church; and the gates of hell shall not prevail against it. [19] And I will give unto thee the keys of the kingdom of heaven: and whatsoever thou shalt bind on earth*

shall be bound in heaven: and whatsoever thou shalt loose on earth shall be loosed in heaven."

Also, in Acts 2:1-4, we read:

"[1] And when the day of Pentecost was fully come, they were all with one accord in one place. [2] And suddenly there came a sound from heaven as of a rushing mighty wind, and it filled all the house where they were sitting. [3] And there appeared unto them cloven tongues like as of fire, and it sat upon each of them. [4] And they were all filled with the Holy Ghost, and began to speak with other tongues, as the Spirit gave them utterance." (See also Acts 2:14-24 & Acts 4:12).

Specifically, in Ephes. 3:9-10), we read:

"9 And to make all men see what is the fellowship of the mystery, which from the beginning of the world hath been hid in God, who created all things by Jesus Christ: 10 To the intent that now unto the principalities and powers in heavenly places might be known by the church the manifold wisdom of God, ..."

The Church is the light of the world. Jesus called those who are His true followers "the Salt of the earth" and "light of the world" (see Matt 5:13-16).

In recent years however, it appears the Church has sold and lost her birthright. Rather than being the salt of the earth and light of the world, which she is and should be, she has blended with the world. Rather than giving direction and guidance to the world and its leaders, she has been taking her bearing from the world. The unfortunate consequence is that God who ought to be at the centre of human existence had become peripheral and an 'add-on' or appendage!

The response of the Church to the issue of sexual perversion and especially homosexuality had been very diverse. In some circles, it has been outright denial that the problem ever existed (at least within their own sects and/or denominations). In some others, the approach has been to be deaf and blind to, or just be silent on the subject. In yet some others, it has been **'see it, hear it, but do nothing about it'**. Such people believe that one way or the other, the problem will die off with time! Of course, in some very special cases there had been an active, a 'zero-tolerance', or a 'no-compromise' stance against the evil of homosexuality & every form of sexual perversion.

The Catholic Church

Like any organization, whether secular or religious, the Catholic Church as a body has had several crises over the years. For example, there was 'historical contradictions' in the area of administrative and spiritual issues, as with the **Medieval Anti-Popes.** There was a time when there were many Popes both in the Vatican and in other parts of the world. The concern then was what would happen in the next world to Catholics who gave their allegiance to the wrong **Pope!** – a question that tormented the consciences in every corner of Christendom [6]. Also, in not too distant past, "the notion of **historical objectivity'** gave way to an essential apologetic approach in which the Catholic Church as a theological concept became inseparable from the actions of its members. This objectivity perhaps made Pope John Paul II, on the eve of the new millennium to take an action unprecedented in the 2000-year history of the Catholic Church – that of calling for 'institutional forgiveness' – the church should become more fully conscious of the sinfulness of her children (recalling all those times in history) when they departed from the spirit of Christ and His Gospel, and indulged in ways of thinking and acting which were truly forms of counter-witness and scandal [7].

Looking at happenings in the Catholic Church, over the years, especially the prevalence of sexual abuses in all and every form - ranging from homosexual practices, Paedophiles, lesbianism, etc., it may be concluded that all these incidences were subtle (though unacceptable) ways in which 'holy' men and 'holy' women tried to express their natural God-given sexual instincts which their oath of celibacy could not succeed in suppressing or destroying. Those among them who did not (or had not) given themselves to these evils, operate as heterosexual priests. As in all evils, homosexuality & other forms of perversion have been finding more and more acceptance and support from the rank and file within the Catholic system and Western society.

The Anglican Church

The Anglican Church is one of the greatest historic pillars of Christianity.

Embraced by greater than 70 million people in over 164 countries, the Anglican Church, not too long ago, faced the real and immediate possibility of collapse. The Church have in the past, had contentious issues such as the divinity of Christ, the ordination of women, discussions about union with other churches, etc. None of these caused a split. However, the issue of homosexuality (& gay marriage) was explosive and today it has ripped the Anglicans apart, putting an end to a century-old and a highly prized international unity. On Sunday 2nd November 2003, an openly homosexual Bishop was consecrated in a small New England College Town. On that day parts of the Anglican Communion decided they could no longer live with one another because there is "a worm in the worldwide apple".

What eventually split the Anglican Church had its foundation or background in a 1991 document **"Issues in Human Sexuality"**. The Paper says in part, 'while under certain circumstances the church should accept lay couples in same-sex relationships, such behavior is unacceptable for ordained ministers'. In 1998, at another Conference in Lambeth, England, the Bishops of the worldwide Communion adopted a resolution that 'all homosexual practice was incompatible with the Scripture'

The Pervasiveness of Evil

For the enemies of truth and righteousness to fill any available space, all they need is just a little space - an entry point. With time, they will take over, overrun, and even displace every trace of truth. That has been the story of the today's Church (John 13:2, 27; Acts 5:1-11). To blind the heart, the devil starts by casting a picture on the mind, then, he diverts that heart gradually but persistently. Soon, he will then fill that heart and mind with its evil, and before you know it, you'll begin to doubt the truth you once cherish, while you also begin to contend its validity. This is what happens to anyone who is overtaken by the spirit of perversion, idolatry and wickedness.

That men, especially leaders of the Catholic and Anglican faith could give in and accept homosexual practice as normal, and even go ahead to ordain and appoint men and women openly known to be involved in these perversions, shows how subtly the enemy has penetrated the Church. A former president of an American Catholic Seminary caused consternation some years back when he suggested that 'perhaps half of those in training for priesthood in American Seminaries were gay'[18].

In his book 'Anglican Church and Homosexuality' (pp 37), Stephen Bates alluded to the fact that within the Anglican Communion, there are two views or schools of thought – the liberal or revisionist, and the traditional view. The liberals believe that the church has authority using, interpreting, and applying Biblical truth, taking into account social changes. This school claims that God's revelation is not complete in what He says in the Bible but evolving and being illuminated through time and circumstances. The traditional view, largely taken by Anglican Evangelicals, places the Bible above the Church, as the ultimate and higher authority rather than the sensibilities of the current church and its leaders. The problem here with the liberal/revisionist school is its limited understanding of the character attributes of the true God of the Bible9! Bishop John Stott, in his 'Same sex partnership? – A Christian Perspective' proceeded squarely with the line: 'modern, loving, homosexual partnership is incompatible with God's created order'. He adds, 'there can be no liberation from God's created norms because true liberation can only be found in accepting them. Homosexuality is a deviation, a fallen disorder'10.

The Catholic Archbishop of Australia, George Pell, has variously (though strongly attacked) declared that 'homosexuality is of a greater health hazard than smoking and that discouraging homosexuality among the young might reduce the number of youth suicide'.[11]

THE CHURCH MUST TAKE A STAND!

To understand the importance of an overwhelming stand of the church against all forms of sexual perversion, especially, homosexuality, lesbianism and gay marriage, on the one hand, and in essence, the gravity or danger of the quietness of the Church on the other, it is important to look at the Church as an institution and recall what roles the founder and Head of the Church, our Lord Jesus, had in mind when He caused what we know today as the Church to be birthed.

The Lord Jesus (and the Disciples who succeeded him), used various terms for the Church and her members. Such terms include 'Salt', 'Light', 'Sheep', 'Saints', etc. The Church has been with us for so long that we have forgotten what the world was like before its presence. It is important to remember that much of the good that we take for granted in modern life has been part of the influence of the Kingdom that Jesus inaugurated. If in our day, it is at least universally acknowledged that sexism, racism and inequality are morally untenable, it is because the church as a community of culturally and socially diverse people

CHAPTER 7

HOMOSEXUALITY - THE DOOM OF NATIONS

Our God is a God of faithfulness, love & mercy. He is also a God of principles. Trends in the Bible, as well as in contemporary times can give us a clue as to what to expect from Him when we obey or disobey His words, or when we breach His principles and laws. For example, in Nehemiah 9:24-31, we read:

> "^{24} So the children went in and possessed the land, and thou subduedst before them the inhabitants of the land, the Canaanites, and gavest them into their hands, with their kings, and the people of the land, that they might do with them as they would. ^{25} And they took strong cities, and a fat land, and possessed houses full of all goods, wells digged, vineyards, and oliveyards, and fruit trees in abundance: so they did eat, and were filled, and became fat, and delighted themselves in thy great goodness. ^{26} Nevertheless they were disobedient, and rebelled against thee, and cast thy law behind their backs, and slew thy prophets which testified against them

to turn them to thee, and they wrought great provocations. ²⁷ *Therefore thou deliveredst them into the hand of their enemies, who vexed them: and in the time of their trouble, when they cried unto thee, thou heardest them from heaven; and according to thy manifold mercies thou gavest them saviours, who saved them out of the hand of their enemies.* ²⁸ *But after they had rest, they did evil again before thee: therefore leftest thou them in the hand of their enemies, so that they had the dominion over them: yet when they returned, and cried unto thee, thou heardest them from heaven; and many times didst thou deliver them according to thy mercies;* ²⁹ *And testifiedst against them, that thou mightest bring them again unto thy law: yet they dealt proudly, and hearkened not unto thy commandments, but sinned against thy judgments, (which if a man do, he shall live in them;) and withdrew the shoulder, and hardened their neck, and would not hear.* ³⁰ *Yet many years didst thou forbear them, and testifiedst against them by thy spirit in thy prophets: yet would they not give ear: therefore gavest thou them into the hand of the people of the lands.* ³¹ *Nevertheless for thy great mercies' sake thou didst not utterly consume them, nor forsake them; for thou art a gracious and merciful God."*

The summary of the above passage of Scriptures is that a flagrant and continued disobedience and breaking of God's laws and principles can not go on indefinitely!

Over the years, the devil had subtly been at work to decimate man - both spiritually and physically. He began it in the Garden of Eden. In these last days, the latest and perhaps the most potent tool he has employed to accelerate his decimation agenda is homosexuality (and it's twin sister Gay marriage)! History shows that individuals, leaders, and Nations who take God for granted and contempt His written Word - the Holy Bible, always ended being doomed. Three forms of doom always befell such individuals, people and/or Nations: it is either God wiped them out (through diseases, pestilences, and or war), or He got them carried far away from their lands - so the land could enjoy a Sabbath and thus be free from further pollution, or He had them replaced by a people who would do His bidding.

God did the first to the seven Nations of Canaanites, the Hivites, the Jebusites, etc, whose lands He later allotted to the Nation of Israel as we know today:

> "^{34} *Then Peter opened his mouth, and said, Of a truth I perceive that God is no respecter of persons:* ^{35} *But in every nation he that feareth him, and worketh righteousness, is accepted with him.* Acts 10:34-35 (see also, Gen 15:18, Deut 7:1-11).

To show that He is no respecter of persons, God did the second to the Nation of Israel - His own very people, too. After several warnings (that they should desist from their idolatrous state), which they refused to heed, God caused their land to be invaded and their wealth carted away. He did not even spare the Temple which He warned King Solomon that He (God) would honour with His presence if the people would also honour Him:

> *"Wherefore the LORD God of Israel saith, I said indeed that thy house, and the house of thy father, should walk before me for ever: but now the LORD saith, Be it far from me; for them that honour me I will honour, and they that despise me shall be lightly esteemed."* (I Sam 2:30)

God sent the king of Babylon to deal with the Israelites, & for seventy good years, they slaved away in Babylon. Psalm 137:1-6 summarizes part of their sorrow in those unforgettable years. Hear them:

> *"[1] By the rivers of Babylon, there we sat down, yea, we wept, when we remembered Zion. [2] We hanged our harps upon the willows in the midst thereof. [3] For there they that carried us away captive required of us a song; and they that wasted us required of us mirth, saying, Sing us one of the songs of Zion. [4]*

How shall we sing the LORD'S song in a strange land? ⁵ If I forget thee, O Jerusalem, let my right hand forget her cunning. 6 If I do not remember thee, let my tongue cleave to the roof of my mouth; if I prefer not Jerusalem above my chief joy."

Not only did God do this to the whole Nation of Israel, he did it to one of their Tribes - the Tribe of Benjamin. God virtually wiped out the entire Tribe because of the sin of sodomy (homosexuality) coupled with the murder that the some of his citizens committed and the murder that followed their wicked acts. In Judges 19:22-25 & 20:28, 34-43,48; 21:15, we read:

> *"²² Now as they were making their hearts merry, behold, the men of the city, certain sons of Belial, beset the house round about, and beat at the door, and spake to the master of the house, the old man, saying, Bring forth the man that came into thine house, that we may know him. ²³ And the man, the master of the house, went out unto them, and said unto them, Nay, my brethren, nay, I pray you, do not so wickedly; seeing that this man is come into mine house, do not this folly.*
>
> *²⁴ Behold, here is my daughter a maiden, and his concubine; them I will bring out now, and humble ye them, and do with them what seemeth good unto*

you: but unto this man do not so vile a thing. ²⁵ *But the men would not hearken to him: so the man took his concubine, and brought her forth unto them; and they knew her, and abused her all the night until the morning: and when the day began to spring, they let her go....* ²⁸ *And Phinehas, the son of Eleazar, the son of Aaron, stood before it in those days,) saying, Shall I yet again go out to battle against the children of Benjamin my brother, or shall I cease? And the LORD said, Go up; for to morrow I will deliver them into thine hand.* ³⁴ *And there came against Gibeah ten thousand chosen men out of all Israel, and the battle was sore: but they knew not that evil was near them.* ³⁵ *And the LORD smote Benjamin before Israel: and the children of Israel destroyed of the Benjamites that day twenty and five thousand and an hundred men: all these drew the sword.* ³⁶ *So the children of Benjamin saw that they were smitten: for the men of Israel gave place to the Benjamites, because they trusted unto the liers in wait which they had set beside Gibeah.* ³⁷ *And the liers in wait hasted, and rushed upon Gibeah; and the liers in wait drew themselves along, and smote all the city with the edge of the sword.* ³⁸ *Now there was an appointed sign between the men of Israel and the liers in wait, that they should make a great flame with smoke rise up out of the city.* ³⁹ *And when the men of Israel* *retired in the battle, Benjamin began to smite and kill of the men of Israel about thirty persons: for they said, Surely they are smitten down before us, as in the first battle. ^{40} But when the flame began to arise up out of the city with a pillar of smoke, the Benjamites looked behind them, and, behold, the flame of the city ascended up to heaven. ^{41} And when the men of Israel turned again, the men of Benjamin were amazed: for they saw that evil was come upon them. ^{42} Therefore they turned their backs before the men of Israel unto the way of the wilderness; but the battle overtook them; and them which came out of the cities they destroyed in the midst of them. ^{43} Thus they inclosed the Benjamites round about, and chased them, and trode them down with ease over against Gibeah toward the sunrising. ^{48} And the men of Israel turned again upon the children of Benjamin, and smote them with the edge of the sword, as well the men of every city, as the beast, and all that came to hand: also they set on fire all the cities that they came to....^{15} And the people repented them for Benjamin, because that the LORD had made a breach in the tribes of Israel."*

The good thing about this great God is that He has not changed (Mal 3:6)! HE - GOD, CAN CLOSE HIS EYES

AND WIPE OUT A MAN, FAMILY, TRIBE AND NATION IF THEY BECOME AND PERSIST IN THEIR WICKEDNESS OF HOMOSEXUALITY AND SAME-SEX MARRIAGE!

Individuals who go into or decide to make homosexuality and gay marriage a way of life, or Are you a leader (both political, religious or corporate), and you are sponsoring Bills, legislating, funding, and promoting this twin evil? Not that you WILL NOT escape the wrath of God!

Of course, when we come to the Church, the consequence is even greater for those who are behind this "Abomination that causes desolation", as earlier prophesied by prophet Daniel (see Daniel 7:11; Matt 24:15; Ezek 32:7; Luke 16:15).

God is at work as ever before. He is wiping out people and nations - through unusual happenings - from strange and incurable diseases, to natural disasters and wars. God is also replacing Nations and lands with peoples from unusual places and colours - something one would never imaginand could happen. Of course, God is also redefining human and topo-geographical map of the world.

This chapter will be incomplete without reference to the Bible story of the people and Cities of Sodom & Gomorrah (Gen 18:20-33, 19:1-5, 24-28). They were so given to the evil of homosexuality and same-sex marriage that the stench of their sin reached Heaven, and God was compelled to execute His written judgment against the Cities. Gen 19:1-11, 24-29 declares:

> *"¹ And there came two angels to Sodom at even; and Lot sat in the gate of Sodom: and Lot seeing them rose up to meet them; and he bowed himself with his face toward the ground; ² And he said, Behold now, my lords, turn in, I pray you, into your servant's house, and tarry all night, and wash your feet, and ye shall rise up early, and go on your ways. And they said, Nay; but we will abide in the street all night. ³ And he pressed upon them greatly; and they turned in unto him, and entered into his house; and he made them a feast, and did bake unleavened bread, and they did eat. ⁴ But before they lay down, the men of the city, even the men of Sodom, compassed the house round, both old and young, all the people from every quarter: ⁵ And they called unto Lot, and said unto him, Where are the men which came in to thee this night? bring them out unto us, that we may know them. ⁶ And Lot went out at the door unto them, and shut the door after him, ⁷ And said, I pray you, brethren, do not so wickedly. ⁸ Behold now, I have two daughters which have not known man; let me, I pray you, bring them out unto you, and do ye to them as is good in your eyes: only unto these men*

do nothing; for therefore came they under the shadow of my roof. ⁹ *And they said, Stand back. And they said again, This one fellow came in to sojourn, and he will needs be a judge: now will we deal worse with thee, than with them. And they pressed sore upon the man, even Lot, and came near to break the door.* ¹⁰ *But the men put forth their hand, and pulled Lot into the house to them, and shut to the door.* ¹¹ *And they smote the men that were at the door of the house with blindness, both small and great: so that they wearied themselves to find the door....*²⁴ *Then the LORD rained upon Sodom and upon Gomorrah brimstone and fire from the LORD out of heaven;* ²⁵ *And he overthrew those cities, and all the plain, and all the inhabitants of the cities, and that which grew upon the ground.* ²⁶ *But his wife looked back from behind him, and she became a pillar of salt.* ²⁷ *And Abraham gat up early in the morning to the place where he stood before the LORD:* ²⁸ *And he looked toward Sodom and Gomorrah, and toward all the land of the plain, and beheld, and, lo, the smoke of the country went up as the smoke of a furnace.* ²⁹ *And it came to pass, when God destroyed the cities of the plain, that God remembered Abraham, and sent Lot out of the midst of the overthrow, when he overthrew the* *cities in the which Lot dwelt."*

The God that dealt summarily with the people and lands of Sodom & Gomorrah has not changed (Mal 3:6). He can, and in fact, He will definitely do the same to & with all promoters of the same sins in our generation!

Are you a leader - either political, industrial, or religious? Or are you an individual who, instead of realizing the distortion Satan has introduced into your mind and body, now think the evil desires & the uncontrollable lust for a person of the same sex is natural and must become a way of life for all? Do you now impose your evil and destructive passion on all around you? God loves you and does not want you to perish. He has made a way of escape via the shed Blood of His Son JESUS Christ. That Blood still cleanses from ALL sins - including all forms of sexual perversion - homosexuality, lesbianism, bestiality, Gay marriage, etc. Hear the word of the Lord:

> *"^{1} There is therefore now no condemnation to them which are in Christ Jesus, who walk not after the flesh, but after the Spirit. ^{2} For the law of the Spirit of life in Christ Jesus hath made me free from the law of sin and death... ^{9} That if thou shalt confess with thy mouth the Lord Jesus, and shalt believe in thine heart that God hath raised him from the dead, thou shalt be saved. ^{10} For with the heart man*

believeth unto righteousness; and with the mouth confession is made unto salvation. ¹¹ For the scripture saith, Whosoever believeth on him shall not be ashamed. ¹² For there is no difference between the Jew and the Greek: for the same Lord over all is rich unto all that call upon him.¹³ For whosoever shall call upon the name of the Lord shall be saved....⁵ This then is the message which we have heard of him, and declare unto you, that God is light, and in him is no darkness at all. ⁶ If we say that we have fellowship with him, and walk in darkness, we lie, and do not the truth: ⁷ But if we walk in the light, as he is in the light, we have fellowship one with another, and the blood of Jesus Christ his Son cleanseth us from all sin. ⁸ If we say that we have no sin, we deceive ourselves, and the truth is not in us. ⁹ If we confess our sins, he is faithful and just to forgive us our sins, and to cleanse us from all unrighteousness. ¹⁰ If we say that we have not sinned, we make him a liar, and his word is not in us."

(Romans 8:1-2; Rom 10:9-13; I John 1:5-10)

If however, you refuse the grace of God, and you persist or die in your sins, BE WARNED, YOU WILL HAVE YOURSELF TO BLAME FOREVER! A Word is enough for the wise. (See Rom 1:28-32; Rom 2:5-11)

CHAPTER 8

THE LIGHT SHINES IN DARKNESS
(JOHN 1:5)

In spite of the desecration and compromises in a section of the Church, the truth is that the Lord Jesus has not changed His mind concerning the role of the Church vis–a-vis His agenda for the world. About His Church, the Lord Jesus said in Matthew 16:16-18:

> *"[16] And Simon Peter answered and said, Thou art the Christ, the Son of the living God. [17] And Jesus answered and said unto him, Blessed art thou, Simon Barjona: for flesh and blood hath not revealed it unto thee, but my Father which is in heaven. [18] And I say also unto thee, That thou art Peter, and upon this rock I will build my church; and the gates of hell shall not prevail against it."*

In the Epistles, the mind of Christ for His Church was further clarified. For example, in Ephesians 3:10:

> *"10 To the intent that now unto the principalities and powers in heavenly places might be known by the church the manifold wisdom of God,..."*

Also, in Ephesians 5: 23-32, Apostle Paul made it clear that Christ is the head of the Church, and that He loved His Church and gave Himself for her. He (Paul), went on that Christ has some expectations from His Church. He expects that the Church would submit totally to Him her head. In the ultimate, Christ would present the Church to God the Father, as a Bride - holy, without spot or wrinkle, or any blemish whatsoever.

There is a good news! There is hope for the Church. All hope is not lost. As we open our mouth wide, feel sorry at the degeneration in the Church today, and perhaps wonder how this could be going on, we must remember the Scriptures in I Cor. 10:11-13:

> *"Now all these things happened unto them for ensamples: and they are written for our admonition, upon whom the ends of the world are come.12 Wherefore let him that thinketh he standeth take heed lest he fall....13 There hath no temptation taken you but such as is common to man: but God is faithful, who will not suffer you to be tempted above that ye are able; but will with the temptation also make a way to escape, that ye may be able to bear it."*

In addition, God still has His remnants within the Church. Despite the invasion of the Church by the twin-evil of homosexuality and gay marriage, and their promoters, there are powerful voices that kept on insisting that righteousness and Biblical standards must be upheld. These men and women remain faithful to the Bible. They are unblending and uncompromising. They refused all coercion and harassment, and would never sell their Birthright. Such few exists even in the Catholic Church. They are also in the Anglican Church and its American counterpart, the Episcopal Church. These group (and we pray that God will multiply them in number and strength), maintain their stand on the infallibility of the Scriptures. They know that all that has been happening are clearly the work of the Devil. They recognize these developments as part of Satan's end-time strategy, an affront on God and His eternal word - the Holy Bible. Among these Disciples of righteousness, we have Bishop Peter Akinola of the Anglican Communion of Nigeria. Bishop Akinola had unequivocally declared that *'Homosexuality is a flagrant disobedience to God, which enables people to pervert God's ordained sexual expression with the opposite sex. In this way homosexuals have missed the mark; they have shown themselves to be trespassers of God's divine laws'*. He continued, *'the practice of homosexuality in our understanding of scripture, is the enthronement of self-will and human weakness and a rejection of God's order and will. This cannot be treated with levity. Otherwise the Church, and the God she preaches will be badly deformed and diminished'*.[13]

What are all these saying to us? God still has His own people as it was in the days of Elijah when all prophets dined and wined with Jezebel on the altar of Baal. God in His greatness, then had reserved over 7000 men who never bowed their knees to or kissed Baal (I Kings 19:18). Today, Bishop Peter Akinola, and other men and women are the tools which God will use to restore the glory that has departed from the house of God.

> "^{4} Then the glory of the LORD went up from the cherub, and stood over the threshold of the house; and the house was filled with the cloud, and the court was full of the brightness of the LORD'S glory....^{18} Then the glory of the LORD departed from off the threshold of the house, and stood over the cherubims. ^{19} And the cherubims lifted up their wings, and mounted up from the earth in my sight: when they went out, the wheels also were beside them, and every one stood at the door of the east gate of the LORD'S house; and the glory of the God of Israel was over them above." (Ezekiel 10:4, 18-19).

A new Response

The truth about homosexuals and all sexual perverts is that they are suffering and burning on the inside. They are enslaved, they long for true love. Even though what they are into is an evil valve, yet they can come out. All they need is a stronger hand:

> "[21] When a strong man armed keepeth his palace, his goods are in peace: [22] But when a stronger than he shall come upon him, and overcome him, he taketh from him all his armour wherein he trusted, and divideth his spoils....[32] And ye shall know the truth, and the truth shall make you free....[36] If the Son therefore shall make you free, ye shall be free indeed....[24] Shall the prey be taken from the mighty, or the lawful captive delivered? [25] But thus saith the LORD, Even the captives of the mighty shall be taken away, and the prey of the terrible shall be delivered: for I will contend with him that contendeth with thee, and I will save thy children. [26] And I will feed them that oppress thee with their own flesh; and they shall be drunken with their own blood, as with sweet wine: and all flesh shall know that I the LORD am thy Saviour and thy Redeemer, the mighty One of Jacob." (Luke 11: 21-22; John 8: 32,36; Isa 49: 24-26).

This is where the Church comes in. As a Church, we have a duty to the errant ones. We are to love them as as part of the people Jesus loved and died for:

> "6 For when we were yet without strength, in due time Christ died for the ungodly. 7 For scarcely for

a righteous man will one die: yet peradventure for a good man some would even dare to die. 8 But God commendeth his love toward us, in that, while we were yet sinners, Christ died for us. 9 Much more then, being now justified by his blood, we shall be saved from wrath through him. 10 For if, when we were enemies, we were reconciled to God by the death of his Son, much more, being reconciled, we shall be saved by his life....19 Nevertheless the foundation of God standeth sure, having this seal, The Lord knoweth them that are his. And, Let every one that nameth the name of Christ depart from iniquity.... 25 In meekness instructing those that oppose themselves; if God peradventure will give them repentance to the acknowledging of the truth; 26 And that they may recover themselves out of the snare of the devil, who are taken captive by him at his will." (Romans 5:6-10; IITim 2:19, 25-26).

We are to intercede for them, particularly that their eyes of understanding be opened (like the prodigal Son in Luke 15:17-20), so they can recognize that they are into what is not convenient.

In truth, homosexuality is an abuse - an abnormal use of the body. It has spiritual, physiological, psychological and emotional consequences. Statistics and Radio interviews proof this. Those whom God is helping not to be entrapped should watch out for Satan's intrigues as well as his intruding agents. One of what has bothered me of recent is the boldness with which some of these shameless men (and women) openly woo people of same sex at Malls, Parks, Train stations etc, in Cities of some so-called Western Nations. It appears Satan has agents, physical and spiritual who are paid to recruit men and especially youths for this evil.

We will also need to take our stand so as not to be partakers in their sins. May I also add very strongly here, that homosexuals should not be allowed to marry each other let alone adopt other people's children. The effects on children so adopted are terrible. It is destructive to their lives and future. It is a cyclical evil which can go on and on for generations.

PART III:

PEACE IN A CONVULSING WORLD

CHAPTER 9

INTER-FAITH DIALOGUES AND WORLD PEACE

For over two decades now (if not more), international focus has been towards Inter-Faith or Multi-faith initiatives. At the core of such initiatives is the search for peace. Many Seminars, Workshops, Tours, Researches, Papers, and Reports have been and are still being put together towards this. It was the belief that if political leaders have failed to bring the world together, and could not also guarantee the protection of lives and properties of innocent citizens in their areas of jurisdiction, it might be good to look somewhere else for peace in our troubled world. Thus religion became a new area of focus. This appears needful when it became clear that 85% of most wars across the world have religious undertone. Also, most, if not all terrorist attacks globally, are traceable to religious fundamentalism being exported abroad from the Middle East, South-East Asia, Latin America and even Africa. Thus, it is felt that if leaders of the world's big religions could come together and understand each other, they will surely be better placed to educate their followers and adherents thereby reducing frictions, conflicts, and even wars. This school has as its basis, the perception or view that the basic cause of much of religious wars and killings is the ignorance of one another's faith. Towards this end, Nations had gone into action. For example, in Australia, this Dialogue was officially 'launched' in March 2003 after 12 months of formal preparation, which was preceded by informal contact and discussions between the National Council of Churches in Australia, Australian Federation of Islamic Councils and the Executive Council of Australian Jewry, etc.

The critical question that needs to be asked is: "How close are we to achieving peace through inter-faith initiatives and efforts? Put differently, it is to be asked: "Has our inter-faith meetings, conferences, communiqués and policies given our world the much peace we are desperately clamoring for? Have they reduced wars, (especially wars that have religion as their real but undeclared basis)? It appears the candid answer to all these questions is a resounding NO!

The Arab Spring in Moslem dominated Nations, The wars in Central African Republic, Syria, South Sudan, North-East of Nigeria, the ISIS, and the terrorist activities the world over, etc, just to mention a few, can all be traced to religious fundamentalism, religious oppression, and intolerance by the government and the governed alike.

What Causes Wars?

The Bible in James 4: 1-2a asks:

> "What is causing the quarrels and fights among you? Isn't it because there is a whole army of evil desires within you? ² You want what you don't have, so you kill to get it. You long for what others have, and can't afford it, so you start a fight to take it away from them."

Also, Jeremiah 17:9 & Matt 15:19 declares:

> "The heart is deceitful above all things, and desperately wicked: who can know it?...For out of the heart proceed evil thoughts, murders, adulteries, fornications, thefts, false witness, blasphemies".

Man's many years of technological breakthrough in several aspects of living have only been able to satisfy his bodily desires and conveniences - all at the expense of his heart and soul. The world is now more dangerous because there are many sophisticated and advanced lethal weapons in the hands of unregenerated souls. Also, human beings are now more difficult to trust and live with than they were years ago. No matter how & where it is practiced - whether simply or in a complicated form, all religions have one major weakness: **they have no power to**

free a man from his sinful nature and life. Only the Blood of Jesus can wash a man's sins away. It is also the only tool that can empower a man not to sin again (Rom 3:23; Rom 6:23; Acts 4:12; I John 1: 5-9).

Peace, Not as the world gives!

In John 14:27, Jesus says:

> *"Peace I leave with you, My peace I give to you; not as the world gives do I give to you. Let not your heart be troubled, neither let it be afraid."*

The goal of inter-faith initiative is world peace. The truth however is that even though over the years, the world and its leaders have been expecting an answer from the mix of inter-faith dialogues, this has never been forthcoming. This may be due to the fact that we have been asking the wrong questions! And, when you go on asking wrong questions, you will continue to get wrong answers! The main questions had been 'What is Peace?', and 'How can we get peace?' Peace has often been defined as 'the absence of war', or 'a state of tranquility or quietness'. It is also said to be 'the lack of friction'. One Dictionary described peace as 'an agreement to end war' and 'a period of time when there is no war or fighting'.

It is in an effort to answer the "how" question, that the concept of 'Inter-faith' dialogue came up. The peace of our

World, and the permanent solution to today's wars, violence, crimes, etc, cannot be found in technology or in ordinary folks or their religious leaders handing down a set of moral code and/or working agreement which they already have in their various 'holy' books.

The Christian Living Bible declares in Hebrews 1: 1-2:

> *"Long ago God spoke in many different ways to our fathers through the prophets, in visions, dreams, and even face to face, telling them little by little about His plans. 2 But now in these days he has spoken to us through His Son to whom He has given everything and through whom He made the world and everything there is."*

We ought to come to that place where we acknowledge and accept the raw truth that Jesus Christ is the Son of God and that HE is - the Messiah sent to the world. We must also understand and acknowledge that He is different from all other religious leaders - both before, and since He came physically into this world.

While physically on this earth, the Lord JESUS spoke and exercised a great & unsurpassed authority. That unique authority and supremacy covered nature (winds and seas, etc). It also covered sicknesses, diseases, demons, all forces of darkness, as well as Satan their master. He was himself subject to the Mighty Name of Jesus (Matt 4:1-11; Matt

8:23-27, Phil 2:5-11). The epitome of that authority was His resurrection from the dead after 3 days:

> "[1] Moreover, brethren, I declare unto you the gospel which I preached unto you, which also ye have received, and wherein ye stand; [2] By which also ye are saved, if ye keep in memory what I preached unto you, unless ye have believed in vain. [3] For I delivered unto you first of all that which I also received, how that Christ died for our sins according to the scriptures; [4] And that he was buried, and that he rose again the third day according to the scriptures: [5] And that he was seen of Cephas, then of the twelve:... [11] Therefore whether it were I or they, so we preach, and so ye believed. [12] Now if Christ be preached that he rose from the dead, how say some among you that there is no resurrection of the dead? [13] But if there be no resurrection of the dead, then is Christ not risen: [14] And if Christ be not risen, then is our preaching vain, and your faith is also vain. [15] Yea, and we are found false witnesses of God; because we have testified of God that he raised up Christ: whom he raised not up, if so be that the dead rise not. [16] For if the dead rise not, then is not Christ raised: [17] And if Christ be not raised, your faith is vain; ye are yet in your sins. [18] Then they also which are fallen asleep in Christ are perished. [19] If in this life only we have

> *hope in Christ, we are of all men most miserable. 20 But now is Christ risen from the dead, and become the firstfruits of them that slept. 21 For since by man came death, by man came also the resurrection of the dead."* (I Cor 15:1-5,13-21).

His bones were not broken and no part of His body is traceable on earth till today because He rose from the dead and ascended into Heaven. After His bodily resurrection, He declared:

> *"All authority in heaven & earth has been given unto Me"* (Matt 28:18-20).

Archaeologists from developed world have dug up graves and searched but could not get at the body of Jesus because He is alive! In Mark 16: 15-18, we read:

> *"[15] And he said unto them, Go ye into all the world, and preach the gospel to every creature. [16] He that believeth and is baptized shall be saved; but he that believeth not shall be damned. [17] And these signs shall follow them that believe; In my name shall they cast out devils; they shall speak with new tongues; [18] They shall take up serpents; and if they drink any deadly thing, it shall not hurt them; they shall lay hands on the sick, and they shall recover."*

No other religion or religious leader has ever made such claims.

One of the names of JESUS is 'THE PRINCE OF PEACE'. Ever before He came physically into this world, God sent forth an advance information in the form of prophecy through one of His Servants, prophet Isaiah:

> *"For unto us a child is born, unto us a son is given: and the government shall be upon his shoulder: and his name shall be called Wonderful, Counsellor, The mighty God, The everlasting Father, The Prince of Peace. ⁷ Of the increase of his government and peace there shall be no end, upon the throne of David, and upon his kingdom, to order it, and to establish it with judgment and with justice from henceforth even for ever. The zeal of the LORD of hosts will perform this"* (Isa 9:6-7).

JESUS is the Prince of Peace! He is the custodian and giver of peace. When He arrives on a scene, it means peace has arrived, and of necessity, war must come to an end. When He declares peace NO one can make war!

What are all these saying? Simply, that the answer to the trauma of our world is in a Person, and not in a 'WHAT'! It is in returning to and seeking the true and living GOD – the God of Heaven and Earth through His Son the Lord Jesus

Christ -The Prince of Peace. We read in Acts 4:12; and Acts 17: 27-31:

> "Nor is there salvation in any other, for there is no other name under heaven given among men by which we must be saved... ^{27} That they should seek the Lord, if haply they might feel after him, and find him, though he be not far from every one of us: ^{28} For in him we live, and move, and have our being; as certain also of your own poets have said, For we are also his offspring. ^{29} Forasmuch then as we are the offspring of God, we ought not to think that the Godhead is like unto gold, or silver, or stone, graven by art and man's device. ^{30} And the times of this ignorance God winked at; but now commandeth all men every where to repent: ^{31} Because he hath appointed a day, in the which he will judge the world in righteousness by that man whom he hath ordained; whereof he hath given assurance unto all men, in that he hath raised him from the dead."

This true and living God has encapsulated all the good things He has in mind for human beings including the much sought-after peace, in the person of His only begotten Son - JESUS CHRIST.

While religion is man's way of finding the True God, Jesus is God's way of finding and returning man back to Himself. Jesus was sent down to earth to show the way to personal peace, community peace and national peace. There has got to be changes that come from the inside of an individual person which will then reflect through his or her actions as well as relationships with his/her environment (- both people and things). Only Jesus can bring about such a change. He can only do it if and when we give Him the chance to.

Perhaps as a person, you are yet to receive Jesus as your personal Saviour and Lord. You must realize that you need Him. He is the only ONE who had done what no religion or any religious leader could ever do for you. Jesus loved you so much that He laid down His very life for you - He became your substitute and took the punishment due to you from God as a result of all your sins! Not only yours but in fact for all the sins of the entire world!:

> "*[21] And she shall bring forth a son, and thou shalt call his name JESUS: for he shall save his people from their sins... [6] For when we were yet without strength, in due time Christ died for the ungodly. [7] For scarcely for a righteous man will one die: yet peradventure for a good man some would even dare to die. [8] But God commendeth his love toward us, in that, while we were yet sinners, Christ died*

for us....²¹ For he hath made him to be sin for us, who knew no sin; that we might be made the righteousness of God in him....¹³ Greater love hath no man than this, that a man lay down his life for his friends....⁵ This then is the message which we have heard of him, and declare unto you, that God is light, and in him is no darkness at all. ⁶ If we say that we have fellowship with him, and walk in darkness, we lie, and do not the truth: ⁷ But if we walk in the light, as he is in the light, we have fellowship one with another, and the blood of Jesus Christ his Son cleanseth us from all sin. ⁸ If we say that we have no sin, we deceive ourselves, and the truth is not in us. ⁹ If we confess our sins, he is faithful and just to forgive us our sins, and to cleanse us from all unrighteousness....¹ My little children, these things write I unto you, that ye sin not. And if any man sin, we have an advocate with the Father, Jesus the righteous: 2 And he is the propitiation for our sins: and not for ours only, but also for the sins of the whole world." (Matt 1:21; Romans 5:6-8; John15:13; II Cor 5:21).

The good news is that no matter how terrible a person is, or how sordid his/her sins may be, Jesus has made provision for all of them to be washed away:

"¹⁸ Come now, and let us reason together, saith the LORD: though your sins be as scarlet, they shall be as white as snow; though they be red like crimson, they shall be as wool....⁵ This then is the message which we have heard of him, and declare unto you, that God is light, and in him is no darkness at all. ⁶ If we say that we have fellowship with him, and walk in darkness, we lie, and do not the truth:⁷ But if we walk in the light, as he is in the light, we have fellowship one with another, and the blood of Jesus Christ his Son cleanseth us from all sin. ⁸ If we say that we have no sin, we deceive ourselves, and the truth is not in us. 9 If we confess our sins, he is faithful and just to forgive us our sins, and to cleanse us from all unrighteousness.... ¹ My little children, these things write I unto you, that ye sin not. And if any man sin, we have an advocate with the Father, Jesus the righteous: ² And he is the propitiation for our sins: and not for ours only, but also for the sins of the whole world." (Is a 1:18; I John 1:5-9; I John 2:1-2)

Peace in the world

Today, Jesus still makes salvation and true peace available to all who believe in His Name (Rom 5:1; Rom 10:9-13; Pro 28:13; Matt 11:28-30). Let me, without mincing words state categorically here that: **IT IS PEACE WITH GOD**

(THROUGH JESUS CHRIST) THAT LEADS TO PEACE WITHIN THE HEART. It is the same peace that will lead to peace in the family, society, AND ULTIMATELY, PEACE IN OUR WORLD.

The peace that JESUS gives when a person invites Him to his or her heart flows from the heart to everyone, everything, and everywhere. That is far, far beyond religion! This peace is like a river - when it flows, it enlarges, and has un-hindered power to engulf the various domains of influence in our Nations, and make our world a great and far better place to live in. Like someone said not too long ago: *'the violence in our world has multiplied. The world has certainly not learned peace, love and cooperation yet. How can it, while the Prince of Peace is universally rejected?'* [14]

A little while ago, I found myself at one of such Inter-faith meetings. It was greatly disgusting to my spirit but it was a learning experience. I believe the Lord led me there so as to let me see the futility of such an exercise. One of the things that provoked my spirit (at the meeting), was the way in which those who represented Christianity were so uncertain of their faith in Jesus. They rambled, and could not present a straight case for any searcher of truth. One particular Reverend of an Orthodox and main line denomination mumbled prayers which he neither started nor ended with the Name of Jesus! It was as if he was afraid to call the most important Name in the whole universe (Phil 2:5-11).

Beloved Reader, Let me close this Chapter by leaving you with these few words to ponder upon:

- The most important event in the history of man is the life, death and resurrection of Jesus Christ.

- The most important understanding in the life of a man is the reality of God and His divine will as given to us through His Holy Word - The Bible (Jer 9: 23-24).

- Of course, the most important decision in the life of any human is the choice he/she must make in regard to personal faith in Jesus Christ15 (Rev 3:20; I John 1:5-9).

CHAPTER 10

A CONVULSING WORLD

The aftermath of an unfruitful rage is confusion! Because the rage of Nations has had no effect on the sovereignty and supremacy of God, as well as His purpose and agenda for the world, the effect is an internal attrition, and a convulsing of the earth's systems.

At a personal level, when you are angry or you are mad at somebody, and he or she looked unruffled, unperturbed, and unmoved, the tendency is for your anger and pressure to rise and you may begin to fume, gallop, and shake all over, even to the extent of convulsing! This is exactly what the world is going through right now. Such a convulsion will definitely birth something - either positive or negative. To the repentant heart who suddenly realizes that he or she has come to his/her wits' end, there will be a cooling down, a quietness that returns him or her to his or her right senses. Like the Prodigal Son (in LUKE 15:17-18), you ask yourself 'why did I rage or get mad in the first place?' You then realize your sinful and helpless state, and return to your Maker and Father (see Rom 3:23; Rom 6:23; Prov 28:13; Isa 55:6-7; I John 1:7-9).

On the other hand, you can decide to let the anger or rage be bottled up inside of you. Then, whoever had the misfortune of crossing your path becomes a victim of your pent up anger. The earth is currently experiencing the same - waiting to birth repentance or the wrath of God! All the wars - whether political, economic, technological, or religious are just preparations for or tastes of what is forthcoming. Also, the floods, typhoons, hurricanes, earthquakes, etc, are just warnings to our world:

> "12 And I beheld when he had opened the sixth seal, and, lo, there was a great earthquake; and the sun became black as sackcloth of hair, and the moon became as blood; 13 And the stars of heaven fell unto the earth, even as a fig tree casteth her untimely figs, when she is shaken of a mighty wind. 14 And the heaven departed as a scroll when it is rolled together; and every mountain and island were moved out of their places. 15 And the kings of the earth, and the great men, and the rich men, and the chief captains, and the mighty men, and every bondman, and every free man, hid themselves in the dens and in the rocks of the mountains; 16 And said to the mountains and rocks, Fall on us, and hide us from the face of him that sitteth on the throne, and from the wrath of the Lamb: 17 For the great day of his wrath is come; and who shall be able to stand?" (Rev 6:12-17).

You can save yourself the heartache of what is around the corner by settling your personal account of sin with God through calling on Jesus for your own salvation. Romans 10:9-13 says:

> "⁹ That if thou shalt confess with thy mouth the Lord Jesus, and shalt believe in thine heart that God hath raised him from the dead, thou shalt be saved. ¹⁰ For with the heart man believeth unto righteousness; and with the mouth confession is made unto salvation. ¹¹ For the scripture saith, Whosoever believeth on him shall not be ashamed. ¹² For there is no difference between the Jew and the Greek: for the same Lord over all is rich unto all that call upon him. ¹³ For whosoever shall call upon the name of the Lord shall be saved."

Make today your own day of salvation, for tomorrow may be too late! II Cor 6:1-2 says:

> "¹ We then, as workers together with him, beseech you also that ye receive not the grace of God in vain. ² (For he saith, I have heard thee in a time accepted, and in the day of salvation have I succoured thee: behold, now is the accepted time; behold, now is the day of salvation)."

CHAPTER 11

IN A TIME LIKE THIS

The Nations are at rage! The world is convulsing and the cosmos are in a state of perplexity. The crossfire is on, news are heart-breaking, and most men are greatly confused. There is fear and hopelessness everywhere. In such a time like this, what should be the attitude, focus and concern of God's true and heaven-minded children?

First, we are not to be afraid and hopeless as the unbelievers or people of the world are. Also, we should not let our faith fail or our heart be troubled. Our love for God and godliness should also remain intact and a priority (Matt 6:33). All these end-time events have been clearly foretold in our Bible. In Chapters 24 and 25 of the Book of Matthew, the Lord Jesus Christ - our Saviour and coming King, had stated that these things must take place. After His Disciples took Him round the Temple at Jerusalem, He gave some of the signs and events that would precede His return. Of the 16 basic things that the Lord said would happen, thirteen (13) had already come to pass!

The times we are in therefore call for gratitude that we have a God who is the Alpha and Omega, the One who knows and declares the end from the very beginning. We are also to rejoice that the return of our Lord is at hand, and our redemption from this self-destruct world is around the corner!

We are, with God's help to be more watchful, more prayerful, and more up and doing. We are to do all we can to witness - warning men of the impending doom - if they will now care to listen.

Above all, we are to be more sensitive to the Holy Spirit so we don't go where He has not sent us, or embark on a journey of no return. Our prayers should be scriptural. We should not be asking God for things that contradict His word and His will for this end time. I Peter 4:7-9 admonished us:

"7 But the end of all things is at hand: be ye therefore sober, and watch unto prayer. 8 And above all things have fervent charity among yourselves: for charity shall cover the multitude of sins. 9 Use hospitality one to another without grudging."

We will do ourselves a lot of good by refraining from being unequally yoked with unbelievers (II Cor 6:14-18). One of the peculiarities of the end-time is the increase (if not multiplication) of false teachers and false doctrines. Hence, we should study God's word so as to know the truth. We are also to stay in obedience to the truth we already know (see John 8:32, 36; John 14:6).

Are you, a 'worldly', 'social' Christian and ceremonial church goer, or an outright Unbeliever? Where do you come in, in all we have been saying so far? You need to urgently wake up from your slumber and face the truth. The Bible says in I Peter 4:18:

> *"If the righteous be scarcely saved, where will the sinner appear in judgment?"*

It is time to be sober and to run for your life! The only safe place to run to is Jesus:

> *"[1] He that dwelleth in the secret place of the most High shall abide under the shadow of the Almighty...[9] Because thou hast made the LORD, which is my refuge, even the most High, thy habitation; [10] There shall no evil befall thee, neither shall any plague come nigh thy dwelling....[28] Come unto me, all ye that labour and are heavy laden, and I will give you rest. [29] Take my yoke upon you, and learn of me; for I am meek and lowly in heart: and ye shall find rest unto your souls. [30] For my yoke is easy, and my burden is light...[20] Behold, I stand at the door, and knock: if any man hear my voice, and open the door"* (Psalm 91:1, 9-10; Matt 11:28-30; Rev 3:20).

May you not be caught unawares!

REFERENCES:

1. Bates, Stephen; 2004, The Church At War – Anglicans and Homosexuality; Tauris & Co Ltd, London.

2. Craughwell, Thomas, J, 2006; Saints Behaving Badly – Doubleday (Random House Inc, New York

3. Duewel, Wesley, L; 2000, More God More Power, Duewel Literature Trust   Inc., Indiana, USA.

4. Enlow, Johnny; 2008, The Seven Mountain Prophecy, Creation House, A   Strange Company, Florida.

5. Keith, D, Lewis;2004: Catholic Church – Legend and Reality,

6. Kenedy, Ted; 2000, Who is Worthy - The Role of Conscience in Restoring   Hope to the Church; Pluto Press Australia Ltd.

7. Maggay, Melba Pedilla; 2004, Institute For Studies in Asian Church and   Culture, Quezon, Philipines.

8. Robinson, V. Gene; 2008; In The Eye of The Storm – Canterbury Press,   Norwich, England.

9. The RCCG, 2011/2012 Sunday School Series; 2011, Directorate of Christian   Education, Abeokuta, Nigeria.

Notes:

Chapter 5

1. RCCG, Sunday School, Sept 2011, pp123-127.

2. Romans 1:24-28, 32.

3. Romans 1:18-23.

4. Enlow, Johnny, pp 83.

Chapter 6

5. Endow, Johnny, pp 83.

6. Craughwell, Thomas, J, pp 20.

7. Keith, D, Lewis Catholic Church – Legend and Reality, pp 1.b

8. The Changing face of Priesthood, Lithurgical Press, 2000, pp20-21.

9. Bates, Stephen, pp 37.

10. Stott, John, Same sex Partnership? – A Christian Perspective, Fleeming H Revel, 1998.

11. Who is Worthy, pp 24-25.

12. Pedilla Maggay, pp 51.

Chapter 8

13. Bishop Akinola, Peter, as quoted in Bates, Stephen, pp16, 37-38.

Chapter 9

14. Grant, R Jeffery, "The Signature of God" (the three points were taken from the book).

Acknowledgements

All you have read so far in this book is clearly through divine inspiration and assistance. I give God all the glory. It is an end-time wake up call. May you the reader, as well as I, the writer, not miss Heaven in Jesus Name. I believe it has blessed you in some way. If so, pass it to others, or better still, buy copies for others both far and near. May we all escape the Divine Rage, and make it Home to Heaven at last.

I thank the many children of God, His and Ministers under whose ministrations and/or writings I have continued to be fed. I also thank all my senior Brothers (Elder Timothy Aderibigbe, Gabriel Adeleke, & Dr. Moses Adedeji - all Haastrups), whose input to my educational life had been used by God to open up several doors to Christian Kingdom & Ministry life. May your own children be great, and affect their generations too for God.

I can not but give great thanks to God for Bro Bayo Adeyokunnu - the friend that introduced me to RCCG. It was a link with destiny! May the Lord bless you and all that are yours in Jesus Name.

The greatest thing that has happened to me in life is my being Born Again. The transformation and the Sprit-led access to the Holy Bible had continued to be my main stay in the thick and thin of life! May what you had received in this book be eternally useful to you.

11/01/2016.

About The Book

In Psalm 2:1, a very critical Question was asked: "Why do the Nations (Heathen) Rage, and the people imagine a vain thing?". The same question came up again in Acts 4:25, apparently quoting from the same book of Psalms. In this book, **'The Nations At Rage'**, additional questions were asked. For instance, what are the Nations and the Heathen raging about, and what has been some of the consequences of their rage? You will surely find deep and probably fearsome answers as you go through. More than the answers, it is our belief that you will personally make peace with God, and if you are already a true child or Minister of God, you will more than ever take your stand in these end times.

About The Author

Abraham Adewole Haastrup is a Pastor in the Redeemed Christian Church of God (RCCG). He read Economics, Public Administration, and Development Finance at the Universities of Ibadan (Nig), Ile-Ife (Nig), and Birmingham (UK) respectively. He also has M.A in Christian Leadership from the West African Theological Seminary (WATS) Lagos, Nigeria.

At present he and his wife Jane Adesola are serving God as Missionaries in Australia/Pacific Region of the RCCG. Christian Mission work has taken Wole Haastrup to Britain, Germany, East Africa, former USSR, and several Pacific Islands. Haastrup has been enabled by God to write some other books (see inside cover). To God be the glory.

www.ingramcontent.com/pod-product-compliance
Lightning Source LLC
Chambersburg PA
CBHW070435010526
44118CB00014B/2057